To the more than fourteen thousand volunteers and dedicated staff of Washed Ashore who have made this project possible —K.C.

Acknowledgments

Special thanks to Angela Haseltine Pozzi, Frank Rocco, and Katie Dougherty at Washed Ashore; Carol Hinz and Jesseca Fusco at Millbrook; Deborah Warren at East West Literary; the Crull clan: April, Alleke, Teo, and Ruben; Dr. Lynn Waterhouse at the Shedd Aquarium; Nina van Zinnicq Bergmann at the Indonesian Waste Platform; Sara Longo with the eXXpedition crew; Carl Berg at Surfrider; Eva Cicoria with Paddle Out Plastic; Carla Isobel Elliff at the University of São Paulo; Katey Valentine at the University of York; Dr. Syma Ebbin at the University of Connecticut; Astrid C. Fischer with the Marine Litter Research Unit, University of Plymouth; Dr. Deborah Rudnick at the Bainbridge Island School District; and Rogier Bos, Todd Bates, Tierney Thys, Marianne Copeland, Sandra Curtis, Alyssa Lefebvre, and Karla Robison.

Millbrook Press™
An imprint of Lerner Publishing Group, Inc.
241 First Avenue North
Minneapolis, MN 55401 USA

For reading levels and more information, look up this title at www.lernerbooks.com.

Image credits: Blue Sky imagery/Shutterstock.com, p. 32; all other images provided by Kelly Crull. Cover image: Kelly Crull.

Designed by Mary Ross.
Main body text set in Mikado. Typeface provided by HVD Fonts.

Library of Congress Cataloging-in-Publication Data

Names: Crull, Kelly, author.
Title: Washed ashore : making art from ocean plastic / Kelly Crull.
Description: Minneapolis : Millbrook Press, [2022] | Audience: Ages 6–10 | Audience: Grades 2–3 | Summary: "Angela Haseltine Pozzi makes animal sculptures from plastic that washes up on beaches. Photos of these sculptures are paired with facts about featured sea creatures and the impacts of plastic on sea life" —Provided by publisher.
Identifiers: LCCN 2021013588 (print) | LCCN 2021013589 (ebook) | ISBN 9781728430300 (library binding) | ISBN 9781728445373 (ebook)
Subjects: LCSH: Pozzi, Angela Haseltine, 1957-–Themes, motives–Juvenile literature. | Refuse as art material–Juvenile literature. | Plastics as art material–Juvenile literature. | Plastic marine debris–Juvenile literature.
Classification: LCC NB237.P72 C78 2022 (print) | LCC NB237.P72 (ebook) | DDC 731/.2–dc23

LC record available at https://lccn.loc.gov/2021013588
LC ebook record available at https://lccn.loc.gov/2021013589

Manufactured in the United States of America
2-1009128-49527-12/14/2022

WASHED ASHORE

Making Art from Ocean Plastic

KELLY CRULL

Ⅿ Millbrook Press · Minneapolis

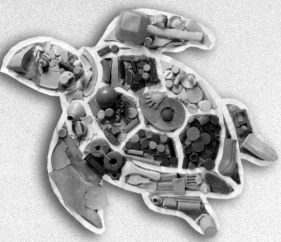

The ocean is home to all kinds of wonderful creatures. Slimy sea slugs. Prickly puffer fish. Glittery grunions. Flashlight fish that glow in the dark. Octopuses that change color if they get scared or grumpy. Dolphins that play tag. Whales that sing so loud they'll rattle your bones.

The ocean is important to all kinds of people too. Some ride its waves. Others explore its depths. Some hunt for food. Others sail on it around the world. While some of us have never even been to the ocean, all of us have left something behind in its waters. Do you know what we've left? Our trash. Every ocean in the world has trash in it. Even a clown fish will tell you that living in a dirty ocean isn't funny, but the worst part is our trash hurts animals. They get tangled up in the trash and can't swim, or they eat the trash because they think it's food. Eating trash can hurt or kill them.

Angela Haseltine Pozzi noticed trash was washing up on the beach near her house and no one was picking it up. Angela had a big idea! But she knew she would need help, so she asked people from her town in Bandon, Oregon, to join her. Together they picked up trash from nearby beaches and used it to make giant sculptures of marine animals at risk because of plastic pollution. The sculptures were so big and beautiful that many people came to see them.

In 2010 Angela and her friends started an organization called Washed Ashore. Their animal sculptures have traveled all over the United States and Canada to visit schools, zoos, aquariums, and museums. They have taught many people about the problem of trash in our ocean. Children have responded by talking to their local city councils, resulting in new laws banning Styrofoam, plastic utensils, and plastic bags from local stores. Students have started recycling programs at their schools. Many people have pledged to never use a plastic bag or disposable water bottle again. Angela says, "Everybody can make a difference. Every action counts!"

In this book, you will find fourteen Washed Ashore sculptures made of ocean plastic. You'll learn fascinating facts about each marine animal as well as tips for how you can reduce plastic pollution. And challenge yourself to find more than eighty different household objects hidden in the sculptures.

LET'S GET STARTED!

PRISCILLA THE PARROTFISH

Most parrotfish live in coral reefs, which look like colorful gardens but are actually made from tiny animals called polyps. Parrotfish clean the coral reefs by eating the algae that grow on them. The parrotfish rip off chunks of dead coral and grind them up to feed on the algae, polyps, and bacteria inside. The dead coral leaves their bodies as sand. In one year, a parrotfish can produce enough sand to fill a sandbox! This sand helps create our beaches.

But parrotfish are losing their homes and food. One reason is that plastic trash rubs against the coral and creates open wounds. Plastic also attracts chemicals, antibiotics, and even viruses. They can infect the coral, and it becomes sick and dies.

Can you find a . . .

bottle

castle

wolf

Leave No Trace

If everyone who visited a beach or wilderness left behind one piece of trash, imagine what that place would look like over time. And imagine how that trash would impact the wildlife that lives there. If everyone picked up one piece of trash instead, these places would become safer and cleaner for everyone.

flip-flop

crab

building block

wrench

STEVE THE WEEDY SEA DRAGON

Did you know dragons exist? Yes, they do! But they breathe bubbles—not fire. They don't even have teeth. Instead, they use their snouts like a straw to suck up tiny crustaceans like mysids and sea lice. They're smaller than a house cat. And they're extremely shy. Still, they have a hidden talent. They are ridiculously good at playing hide-and-seek. Sea dragons are nearly impossible to see, even if you are looking straight at them. They blend in perfectly with the seagrass and kelp forests where they live. But our trash is destroying their perfect hiding spot. We can help protect sea dragons by keeping our beaches clean, so our trash does not reach their homes near the shore.

Can you find a . . .

turtle

soda bottle

tugboat

Get the Cone

The next time you enjoy ice cream at the beach or another favorite spot, choose to eat your ice cream in a cone. By not using a cup or a plastic spoon, you make less trash. Besides, who needs a cup when you can eat the cone?

chain

bubble blower

flashlight

carabiner

OCTAVIA THE GIANT PACIFIC OCTOPUS

The giant Pacific octopus is one of the most intelligent creatures in the ocean. It can solve problems, use tools, and communicate by changing colors. These octopuses make dens in rocks near the shore. From their hideouts, they use eight arms lined with suckers to lasso prey, mainly shrimp, clams, lobsters, and fish.

Most plastic enters the ocean from the coast. It can easily get trapped in the rocks where the octopuses live. Some octopuses make their dens in plastic containers that may carry poisonous chemicals or germs. Broken plastic with jagged edges can injure them. Some octopuses have been observed hiding in clear plastic containers, unaware that their prey and predators can easily see them. Maybe it's time to look for a new hiding spot!

Can you find a . . .

goose

buoy

shrimp

Buy It Used

New products must be made, packaged, and shipped. They use resources and produce waste. When possible, shop at thrift stores and buy used items rather than new ones. Even better, borrow what you need from a friend or neighbor. When you're finished with your things, sell them or pass them along to someone who needs them.

cooler

seahorse

stereo

rake

ZORABELLE THE ROCKHOPPER PENGUIN

Most people will never have the chance to observe a rockhopper penguin in the wild. They live near Antarctica on some of the most remote islands in the world. Believe it or not, even these distant shores are littered with plastic. When our trash enters the ocean, powerful rotating currents called gyres—think of them as enormous whirlpools—carry our trash around the world. A plastic bottle might enter the ocean in New York and wash ashore next to a rockhopper penguin. Plastic has been found on the rocky shores where these penguins live and in the water where they hunt. Plastic has even been found in the krill and small crustaceans they eat.

Can you find a . . .

propeller

crocodile

spoon

Let's Get This Party Started

Be creative when you ask or look for a gift. Choose a gift made from natural materials like a craft, painting, wooden toy, or favorite food. Or consider putting on a magic show, building a fort together, or going on a camping trip. By doing so, you've also given a gift to your friends in the ocean by keeping their homes free of more plastic.

stake

fish-finder

marker

sprayer

AMERICA THE SEA STAR

Maybe you've heard them called starfish, but sea stars are not actually fish. They do not have gills, scales, fins, or a backbone as fish do. There is something fishy about sea stars, though. They eat inside out. Their stomach comes out of their mouth, eats food, and goes back inside. Thank your lucky stars you're not one of their favorite foods: mollusks, oysters, and snails. Sea stars populate every kind of marine habitat, including tidal pools, rocky shores, seagrass, kelp forests, and coral reefs.

Most plastics in the ocean eventually break up into tiny pieces called microplastics. Some fall to the ocean floor. Sea stars that live a mile (1.6 km) beneath the surface of the sea have been found with microplastics in their stomachs. These microplastics may cause them to grow more slowly and lay fewer eggs.

Can you find a . . .

shotgun shell

golf ball

tire

What Goes Up, Must Come Down

Many balloons are made of plastic. Wind can carry loose balloons thousands of miles in a single day. Many end up in the ocean. Celebrate a better way! Blow bubbles, fly a kite, doodle with chalk, or make paper or flower chains.

lighter

bottle cap

shoe sole

fishing lure

NORA THE SALMON

Salmon can live in both fresh and salt water. They hatch in fresh water where they eat insects and small crustaceans. Most salmon swim to the sea. They mainly eat fish to grow big and strong. As adults, they face their biggest challenge—the salmon run. They return to the river where they were born, sometimes thousands of miles, to lay eggs, which is called spawning. They swim against the current, and some leap as high as 12 feet (3.7 m) to climb waterfalls and dams. They dodge hungry bears and eagles. Because of the effort required to complete this journey, most die within weeks of spawning.

Each year millions of pounds of plastic also travel down streams and rivers to the ocean. These plastics can come from unlikely sources. For instance, did you know car tires contain plastic? They are a major source of microplastics in the ocean. Tires also contain a chemical that can kill salmon.

Can you find a . . .

toothbrush

squirt top

inhaler

Clean It Up

Challenge yourself to pick up at least one piece of trash each day on your walk to school, to the playground, or through your neighborhood. Even if you don't live near water, you can stop plastic from reaching the ocean by picking it up on land.

handle

motorcycle

pen

spool

BLUEBERRY THE SEA JELLY

Sea jellies have no bones, heart, lungs, or brain. And get this, sea jellies eat and poop out of the same hole!

Their simple design is their advantage. Sea jellies can thrive anywhere. They live in the warm tropics and the icy Arctic, near the surface and on the seafloor. They eat fish, shrimp, crabs, tiny plants, and even other jellies. Some host algae that use photosynthesis to make food for them—like plants. They can do it all!

Sea jellies are so good at collecting plastic that humans can use their slime to filter microplastics out of sewers. What stinks is that sea jellies are a popular snack for many animals. Let's say a shark eats a sea lion that ate a sunfish that ate a sea jelly. These animals digest the food, but the plastic can stay inside them and travel up the food chain.

Can you find a . . .

shovel

toothbrush

buoy

Say No to Plastic Bags

Plastic bags easily catch the wind and end up in waterways that lead to the ocean. Plastic bags in the water look and move like sea jellies. Hungry animals can't tell the difference and eat plastic bags by mistake. To help save our ocean creatures, use reusable bags whenever possible.

cleaner

ball

bobber

water bottle

EDWARD THE LEATHERBACK SEA TURTLE

The leatherback sea turtle is named for its shell, which is soft like a leather shoe. Leatherbacks are the largest turtles in the world. They can grow up to 7 feet (2 m) long and weigh 2,000 pounds (907 kg)! They spend most of their lives in the open ocean and travel as many as 10,000 miles (16,000 km) each year making them one of the most highly migratory animals. Because leatherbacks mostly eat sea jellies, they often eat plastic bags by mistake. Plastic bags can block their intestines, preventing them from digesting food.

Can you find a . . .

remote control

sunglasses

hot drink lid

Skip the Straw

Plastics made to be used only once are called single-use plastics. For example, plastic straws are used once but last hundreds of years. When you order a drink at a restaurant, ask for no straw—or bring your own reusable straw!

jug

pump

lighter

pacifier

CHOMPERS THE TIGER SHARK

Tiger sharks are called the garbage cans of the sea. That's because they will try to eat almost anything. Their prey includes fish, seabirds, dolphins, sea turtles, rays, crustaceans, and even other tiger sharks. But they have been found with tires, license plates, a chicken coop, a bag of money and, you guessed it, plastic in their stomachs! While they are found in many different marine habitats, they prefer to feed near the shore where most of our trash enters the sea. Tiger sharks are tough, but sharp edges from garbage can damage their organs, resulting in death.

Can you find a . . .

calculator

fencing

action figure

Snack on Fresh Foods

Food wrappers are one of the most common types of trash in the ocean. On your next outing, bring along an apple, banana, or carrot sticks instead of a packaged snack. Fresh foods are healthy, fill you up, and need no wrapper.

surfboard fin

umbrella handle

spoon

soldier

COSMO THE TUFTED PUFFIN

Tufted puffins spend most of their lives at sea. They sleep on the surface of the water and only come ashore to breed. They are diving birds and swim with their wings underwater while catching fish. They are one of the only birds that can hold ten or more fish in their mouths at once. Puffins also like to peck at food left on plastic trash. They end up eating the plastic too. Their stomachs fill up with plastic, which they can't digest. They become weak and are eaten or starve. Unfortunately, puffins will even feed plastic to their chicks.

Can you find a . . .

hair pick

rice paddle

hook

Plan Ahead

When you eat out, say no to plastic plates, tableware, cups, lids, straws, and takeout boxes. Ask for paper or aluminum foil, or bring your own supplies. Send an email or write a letter to a favorite restaurant asking them to use less plastic. Say thank you to those restaurants that already reduce their use.

knife handle

lip balm

spoon

hairbrush

DAISY THE POLAR BEAR

Polar bears are the largest land carnivores. They live in the Arctic and primarily eat seals, which they can smell from nearly a mile (1.6 km) away. Polar bears can't swim as fast as seals, so they depend on sea ice as a hunting platform. Seals cut breathing holes in the ice, and when they pop up for air, the bears snatch the seals with their enormous paws. Other times, seals relax on the ice, giving polar bears a chance to sneak up and kill them.

Arctic sea ice is disappearing due to climate change. We produce more than 380 million tons (345 million t) of plastic each year. That's roughly the weight of the entire human population. Plastic production and disposal require burning fossil fuels, which create greenhouse gases. These gases trap energy from the sun in the atmosphere and accelerate climate change. As the Arctic warms, sea ice melts, and more polar bears die of starvation.

Can you find a . . .

pill bottle

measuring spoon

lens cap

lion

flower

wheel

nasal spray

LIDIA THE SEAL

Seals are excellent divers. The elephant seal, for example, can hold its breath underwater for two hours. Seals can be found throughout the world, though most live in polar seas. Their diet consists mainly of fish, squid, and crustaceans such as crabs, shrimps, and lobsters.

Seals and other marine animals often get entangled in ropes, straps, and nets. If they can't move, they starve or drown. If they live, the plastic cuts into their skin as they grow.

Look closely at the items used to make Lidia's skin. Can you guess how she got her name?

Can you find a . . .

hard hat

mask

monster truck

Pay Attention to Packaging

Buy in bulk and without packaging when possible. If that's not an option, choose products packaged in glass or paper instead of plastic. Glass is infinitely recyclable. Most paper can be recycled six or seven times. Plastics labeled #1 PET and #2 HDPE are best, but most plastic is not recyclable.

jug

bottle top

water bottle

training wheel

GRACE THE HUMPBACK WHALE

Humpback whales swim through every ocean in the world. They eat up to 2,000 pounds (907 kg) of krill, plankton, and small fish every day. Not long ago, however, they were hunted almost to extinction. To protect these animals, commercial whaling was banned in most countries in 1986.

These whales represent one of the greatest comeback stories in the ocean. More than half the humpback whale populations have recovered, and they are no longer considered endangered species. It's a good start!

This whale's next greatest threat may be our trash. They get tangled up in fishing gear that fishers have left behind or are using to catch other animals. We can ensure a bright future for these whales by working together to solve the problem of plastic pollution.

Can you find a . . .

hanger

steering wheel

shoe

fish

visor

buckle

pipe

SCAVENGER HUNT

Plan a visit with friends and family to your favorite beach or waterway, such as a lake, river, or pond, to collect plastics. Here are a few tips from the volunteers at Washed Ashore:

1. **Pick a Date and Time**

   Choose a day when you will be free, such as a weekend. Check the weather forecast in advance. If you're headed to the beach, low tide is safest and more of the beach is visible. Decide how to dispose of the plastics you collect. Recycle and repurpose what you can and dispose of the rest safely. If you use a trash can, secure the lid, so the plastic doesn't end up back in the ocean.

2. **Spread the Word**

   Invite your family and friends to join the hunt. Ask them to bring friends, coworkers, and classmates. Explain that every piece of plastic they pick up and dispose of properly will stay out of the ocean. Every action counts!

THINGS TO LOOK FOR . . .

Toys
What could possibly be better than free toys? Keep an eye out for bath toys, dolls, trucks, action figures . . . even unicorns.

Balls
Play a pickup game with a ball that has washed ashore or a game of catch with a friendly dog.

Plastic Jewels
Imagine the smaller pieces of plastic are jewels of every shape and color. At home, drill holes in them and put them on a string to make a necklace.

3. Gather Supplies

Remind everyone to bring garden gloves to protect their hands and reusable bags or buckets for collecting plastic. Soap and vinegar will disinfect any items you plan to repurpose.

4. Be Safe

Find out who owns the property and if there are any restrictions or safety measures you need to follow. Read signs and be aware of high tides and currents. Collect during low tides and far from the shoreline. Watch out for slippery rocks, driftwood, and sea life.

5. Hunt for Plastic

Look for smaller pieces of plastic along the wrack line—the line of seaweed, driftwood, and shells left on the beach at high tide. Bigger pieces of plastic are often found among rocks, logs, or grassy areas.

6. Keep a Field Journal

Count all the different types of plastic you find, and keep a record in a field journal or use an app like Litterati. Ask local scientists if they are interested in what you find, especially if you hunt for plastic regularly. Many scientists rely on this kind of information to improve our understanding of plastic pollution.

7. Have Fun!

Hunting for plastic is hard work, so make it fun. Give a prize to the person who collects the most plastic or who finds the most unusual piece of plastic. When you finish, wash up and celebrate. Sit down for a snack and thank everyone for coming to help.

Rope
Anyone up for a game of tug-of-war? Pick the strongest and longest piece of rope you can find, divide into teams, and let the games begin!

Bottle Caps
See if you can find a bottle cap for every color of the rainbow, even purple, which is often the hardest to find.

Harmful Objects
Ask an adult for help disposing of sharp objects and bottles that may contain dangerous fluids.

BUILDING THE SCULPTURES

Angela and the Washed Ashore volunteers show how they make a sculpture of a sea turtle out of ocean plastic.

1 Geek Out

Angela wants to learn everything she can about sea turtles. She reads, watches videos, interviews experts, and looks at pictures in books and online. She prints her favorites and hangs them in her studio.

2 Sort the Plastics

Angela sorts through the plastics collected by the Washed Ashore volunteers. She looks for pieces with shapes, colors, and textures that remind her of a sea turtle. The pieces she saves are washed and trimmed by her staff.

3 Fit the Pieces Together

Volunteers use bendy wire and screws to attach the plastic pieces to panels made out of metal mesh. The panels fit together like puzzle pieces to create the outer shell of the sea turtle. Angela takes special care to find just the right pieces for the eyes, mouth, and flippers.

4 Build the Frame

Welders use stainless steel rods to construct the skeleton of the sea turtle. They bend the rods and weld them together. Like our skeletons, the metal frame is built to carry the weight of the outer shell and withstand travel.

5 Attach the Plastic to the Frame

The last step is to attach the plastic pieces to the frame with wire and screws. The animal's personality starts to emerge, and Angela gives it a name. After six to eight months of hard work, the sculpture is complete. The volunteers celebrate by sending off the sea turtle to meet kids at zoos, aquariums, and museums all over the country.

MAKE YOUR OWN

You can also create art to save the sea. Collect plastics from outside or from your recycling bin. Wash and sort them by shape and color. Outline your favorite marine animal with masking tape, sidewalk chalk, or sticks. Fill in the marine animal with the plastics. Try different combinations until you find one you like.

Share your artwork with friends and family. Use the information from this book to tell them about plastic in the ocean.

WHERE DO PLASTIC BOTTLES GO?

You need a drink of water, so you drink from . . .

the tap
Congratulations! Drinking tap water is healthier for you, saves resources, and reduces waste and pollution. Wasn't that easy?

a single-use water bottle

To produce the water bottle, companies . . .

extract oil from the ground

transform the oil into plastic pellets

heat and shape the pellets into bottles

a reusable bottle
It's your best option on the go, but you still need to dispose of the bottle when it wears out.

The amount of water required to produce a 16 oz (0.5 L) water bottle could be up to seven times what's inside the bottle.

Bottles are packaged and transported to your local store.

One million water bottles are sold every minute.

When you're finished . . .

you throw it away

you recycle it
Even though you recycle, only one out of every six plastics actually gets recycled. Most still end up in a landfill.

Your plastic bottle is made into new products like containers, lumber, carpet, pipes, clothes, and playground equipment.

in a trash can
where a garbage truck will haul it away to

a landfill
where your water bottle decomposes for 450 years

an incinerator
where it is burned to generate electricity to power homes but also produces harmful greenhouse gases

in the street
Your bottle is blown or washed into a waterway or storm drain that empties into the ocean.

Every minute, one truckload of plastic enters the ocean.

In the ocean, your water bottle . . .

is eaten by a marine animal
causing starvation, blocked intestines, or internal injury

entangles a marine animal
and if they can't break free, they starve, drown, or get hurt

litters a beach or other ocean habitat
often destroying the homes of the animals that live there

breaks down into microplastics
that enter the food chain and may carry harmful chemicals and impact bodily functions of animals

GLOSSARY

antibiotic: a medicine that is used to cure infections and kill bacteria that make you sick

carnivore: an animal that eats primarily or only meat

crustacean: a group of animals such as crabs, lobsters, and shrimp that mostly live in water, have several pairs of legs, and a body made up of sections that are covered with a hard shell

digest: to change food into simpler forms that can be used by the body

fossil fuel: a fuel such as coal, oil, or natural gas that is formed in the ground from dead plants or animals over a long time

greenhouse gases: gases in Earth's atmosphere such as carbon dioxide, methane, and water vapor that trap energy from the sun. Without these gases, the planet would be too cold for life. Humans produce greenhouse gases, which trap energy in the atmosphere and cause climate change.

gyre: a system of rotating ocean currents, caused by wind patterns and the rotation of Earth, that collects a large amount of plastic waste at its center

krill: a tiny crustacean similar to shrimp that lives in the ocean and is the main food source of some whales

microplastics: tiny bits of plastic less than 0.2 inches (5 mm) long that can be harmful to living things. Glitter is an example of a microplastic.

migratory: a fish, animal, or bird that moves from one place to another at certain times of the year in search of warmer weather, food, or a place to breed

photosynthesis: how green plants use carbon dioxide, water, and sunlight to make their own food

polyp: a small tube-shaped sea animal with one end attached to a rock or other surface and a mouth lined with stinging tentacles at the other end

recycle: to make something new from something that has been used, such as making new carpet out of used plastic water bottles

repurpose: to use something for a different purpose from which it was originally used such as using plastic bags from the store to line trash cans at home

spawning: to lay and fertilize eggs in water

tidal pool: a pool of water left behind when the tide goes out that becomes a home for small sea animals and plants; also called a tide pool

A VAST SEA OF KNOWLEDGE

Dive into a Book

Andrus, Aubre. *The Plastic Problem: 60 Small Ways to Reduce Waste and Help Save the Earth*. Oakland: Lonely Planet Kids, 2020.

Barr, Catherine. *A Turtle's View of the Ocean Blue*. Illustrated by Brendan Kearney. London: Laurence King, 2021.

Beer, Julie. *Kids vs. Plastic: Ditch the Straw and Find the Pollution Solution to Bottles, Bags, and Other Single-Use Plastics*. Washington, DC: National Geographic Kids, 2021.

Blom, Kirsti, and Geir Wing Gabrielson. *Plastic Sea: A Bird's-Eye View*. Edited by Brian Scott Sockin. Translated by Helle Valborg Goldman, Apex, NC: Cornell Lab, 2020.

French, Jess. *What a Waste: Rubbish, Recycling, and Protecting Our Planet*. London: DK Children, 2019.

Kim, Eun-ju. *Plastic: Past, Present, and Future*. Translated by Joungmin Lee Comfort. London: Scribe, 2019.

Newman, Patricia. *Plastic, Ahoy! Investigating the Great Pacific Garbage Patch*. Illustrated by Annie Crawley. Minneapolis: Millbrook Press, 2014.

Surf the Web

International Coastal Cleanup
https://oceanconservancy.org/trash-free-seas/international-coastal-cleanup/
Find and join a cleanup at a lake, river, or beach near you. Or make a splash by planning your own cleanup following the website's simple instructions.

Leave No Trace
https://lnt.org/why/7-principles/
Learn seven principles that will help you take care of our planet whenever you are outdoors, whether you're on a camping trip, at the park, or in your backyard.

Monterey Bay Aquarium
https://montereybayaquarium.org
Get your feet wet with online classes, crafts, printables, and live cams featuring your favorite marine animals. Help turn the tide on plastic pollution by following the suggestions on their "Act for the Ocean" page.

***National Geographic Kids*: Kids vs. Plastic**
https://kids.nationalgeographic.com/nature/kids-vs-plastic
Reduce the amount of plastic you use with tips from *National Geographic Kids* on everything from planning a party to finding a gift to choosing your next snack.

Smithsonian: Marine Plastics
https://ocean.si.edu/conservation/pollution/marine-plastics
If you're doing a project about marine plastics for school, the Smithsonian is a great jumping-off point. Take a deep dive into a wide range of topics related to ocean plastic with in-depth facts, charts, and videos.

Washed Ashore
https://washedashore.org
Visit Washed Ashore online to see more than eighty marine animal sculptures. If you would like to make your own art from ocean plastic at school, tell your teacher about the free Integrated Arts Marine Debris Curriculum.

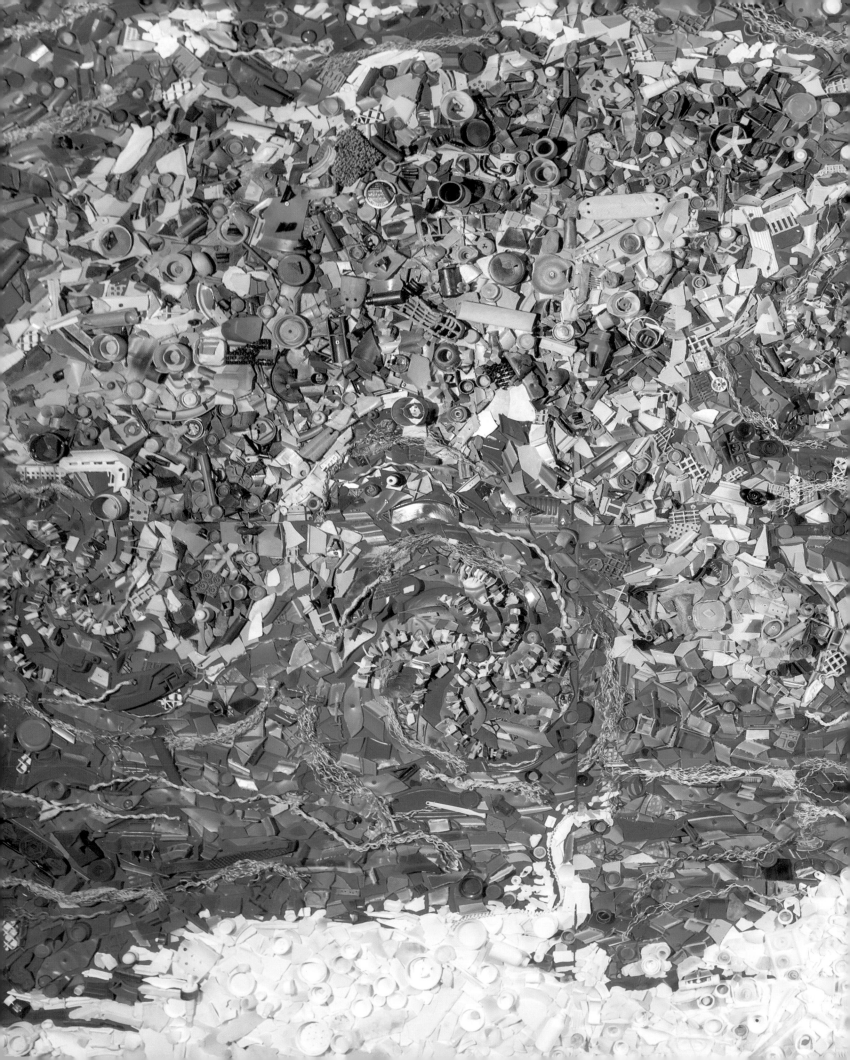